BOSTON LIGHT

The First Lighthouse in North America

AILEEN WEINTRAUB

The Rosen Publishing Group's
PowerKids Press™
New York

To my mom, for leaving the light on

Published in 2003 by The Rosen Publishing Group, Inc.
29 East 21st Street, New York, NY 10010

First Edition

Editors: Leslie Kaplan and Jennifer Landau
Book Design: Maria E. Melendez

Photo credits: Cover and title page photo © Mark Hunt/Index Stock; p. 4, p. 7 all, p. 12, p. 13 top right, p. 16, p. 17 top right, p. 19, p. 21 top right © United States Lighthouse Society; p. 8 U.S. Coast Guard official photo; p. 10 top left © Archivo Iconografico, S.A./CORBIS; p. 11 © Bettmann/CORBIS; p. 15 © Frank Siteman/Index Stock; p. 20 © Rick Hornick/Index Stock; p. 22 bottom right © Kindra Clineff/Index Stock; cover, title page, background, and border illustrations by Maria Melendez.

Weintraub, Aileen, 1973–
      Boston Light : the first lighthouse in North America / Aileen Weintraub.
        p. cm. — (Great lighthouses of North America)
      Includes bibliographical references and index.
      Summary: This is a history of the first American lighthouse, which was built at the entrance to Boston Harbor in 1713.
      ISBN 0-8239-6170-2 (lib. bdg.)
      1. Boston Light (Mass.)—Juvenile literature   [1. Boston Light (Mass.) 2. Lighthouses] I. Title II. Series
      VK1025.B6 W45 2002   2001-003896
      387.1'55'0974461—dc21

Manufactured in the United States of America

Contents

1 Little Brewster Island   *5*

2 A Rich History   *6*

3 Shipwrecks!   *9*

4 Through the Wars   *10*

5 A New Lighthouse   *13*

6 A History of Light   *14*

7 Keeping the Light   *17*

8 A Dangerous Job   *18*

9 Ghost Stories   *21*

10 The Coast Guard Takes Over   *22*

     Glossary   *23*

     Index   *24*

     Web Sites   *24*

Little Brewster Island is one of more than 30 islands in Boston Harbor.
It is a very small island.

Little Brewster Island

Boston Light is a lighthouse at the entrance of Boston Harbor. Lighthouses are towers with bright lights on top. They are built along coastlines around the world to help guide ships through rough weather and oceans. Boston Light shines its light from Little Brewster Island, 2 miles (3 km) east of Massachusetts Bay. In the 1600s, trade ships sailed the main **channel** near Little Brewster Island. Many ships were wrecked on jagged rocks in the small **inlets**. When the ships sank, the goods they carried also sank and the people on board sometimes drowned. Merchants made a living by selling or trading goods. If a ship carrying valuable goods sank, then a merchant lost business. In 1713, Boston merchants convinced the Massachusetts colonial **legislature** to build a lighthouse on Little Brewster Island.

A Rich History

Boston Light is famous for being the first lighthouse built in North America. It is also famous for being the last lighthouse in the country that is still manned, or run by people. Boston Light was completed in 1716. From the bottom of its **foundation** to the top of its roof, it measures 75 feet (23 m). The original lighthouse was a stone tower.

Before there were lighthouses, people set signal fires in certain areas to provide guiding lights for ships. Today ships have modern **navigational** systems and do not need to rely on lighthouses. However, Boston Light continues to operate and to guide ships. This first American lighthouse has even been named a national **landmark**. National landmarks are very important historical sites that are carefully preserved.

Top: *Steel bands fastened around Boston Light to support it can be seen here.*
Bottom: *A cannon was placed near Boston Light in 1719, to serve as a fog signal.*

Before Boston Light was built to help guide British merchant ships to safety, ships often crashed on the rocky shores of Massachusetts.

Shipwrecks!

In the 1700s, sailing a ship in any ocean was a dangerous job. Ships often crashed into rocks and **sandbars** beneath the water. Once a ship was stranded, powerful waves could break it apart. The cold water in Boston Harbor made it impossible for sailors from wrecked ships to survive for very long. Stormy weather often kept rescuers from reaching sailors who were drowning. Nearly 120 shipwrecks have occurred in and near Boston Harbor. The beam of Boston Light cannot always be seen through fog. To help guide ships through fog, a cannon was placed near the lighthouse in 1719. When sailors heard the cannon fire, they knew how far they were from land. Fog signals such as bells, whistles, and horns came to replace the cannon.

Through the Wars

Boston Light did not fare well during the American Revolution. In July 1775, American colonists set fire to the wooden parts of their own lighthouse so the British couldn't use its light to enter the harbor. The British tried to fix the damage, but General George Washington sent men to stop them. In June 1776, the British were forced to sail out of Boston Harbor. They blew up the lighthouse, and a new one had to be built. The American Revolution wasn't the only war to affect the use of Boston Light. During the **War of 1812** and World War I (1914–1918), the new tower's lamps were dimmed. During World War II (1939–1945), they were turned off. Since 1945, the tower has been lit.

George Washington was commander in chief of the Colonial armies in the American Revolution (1775–83).

George Washington led his men across the Delaware River into New Jersey, where they surprised and defeated enemy troops in December 1776.

The keepers at Boston Light climbed around and around stairs such as these to reach the enclosed glass lantern that tops the lighthouse.

A New Lighthouse

After the American Revolution, construction began on a new lighthouse. In 1783, the state of Massachusetts funded the building of the lighthouse that stands today. It stands on the same spot as did the original. The new Boston Light was built of stone and brick. In 1809, dangerous cracks appeared in the tower. Six heavy, iron bands were placed around the lighthouse for support. In 1844, **cast-iron** stairs replaced the wooden ones. In 1851, a bell replaced the cannon as a fog signal. In 1859, the tower was raised 14 feet (4 m) to its present height of 89 feet (27 m). This was done to make room for a new lens in the tower, called a **Fresnel lens**.

Cracks in a lighthouse cannot be ignored, or the entire building might fall down.

13

A History of Light

At the start of the eighteenth century, lighthouses around the world were lit by candles. Later the light came from oil-burning lamps. In 1811, Argand lamps were placed in Boston Light. These lamps used **kerosene**, which did not give off smoke and fumes. Argand lamps also used **reflectors**, which helped to create a strong beam of light. In 1859, the lighthouse was fitted with a lens invented by Augustin Fresnel. The Fresnel lens uses glass **prisms** to **magnify** and bend light into a steady beam. In 1948, electricity was **installed** in the tower. Today the light can be seen for 27 miles (43.5 km). It flashes once every 10 seconds and has a **candlepower** of almost 2 million.

A Fresnel lens (above) looks something like a glass beehive.
The Fresnel lens at Boston Light is made of 336 pieces of glass.

The keeper's assistants at Boston Light lived in the house shown above, which was built in the colonial revival style.

Keeping the Light

Keepers lived on Little Brewster Island with their families until the 1960s. Since 1854, each main lighthouse keeper has had two assistants. Before the discovery of electricity, the keeper had a very busy job. Keepers poured fuel for the tower lamps into cans. Then they carefully carried the cans to the **lantern** room. The keepers also had to clean the **soot** from the lamps, polish all the brass work, trim the wicks, and wind the gears that turned the light. If the weather was foggy, they operated the fog signal as well. Keepers also kept a lookout for ships that might be in trouble.

Glass surfaces in the lantern room were cleaned very well to let the light travel through.

17

A Dangerous Job

The first keeper of Boston Light was George Worthylake. In 1718, two years after Worthylake took his post, a terrible accident happened. Worthylake was on his boat with his wife, his daughter, and their slave, Shadwell. Worthylake's boat sank, and everyone on board drowned. Months later Worthylake's replacement, Robert Saunders, also drowned in a boating accident.

More than 60 keepers have worked at Boston Light, and all have been men. In the 1700s and 1800s, many of the jobs open to men were not open to women. The keepers' wives and daughters worked very hard at the lighthouse, though. The wives kept everything clean, raised the children, and assisted their husbands.

A triple marker was placed over the graves of the Worthylakes. It reads, "George, in his forty-fifth year, Ann in her fortieth, and Ruth, their daughter."

Few changes have been made to the structure of Boston Light since it was rebuilt in 1783, but its lighting gear has improved steadily.

Ghost Stories

Boston Harbor can be a very foggy place. There is a certain area known as Ghost Walk that stretches around Little Brewster Island for several miles. It is said that no foghorn can be heard in this area, no matter how loud it is. In 1893, university students did experiments to reach this area with the sound of a foghorn. Not one person succeeded. This remains a mystery today. Some keepers have reported strange events on Little Brewster Island. Dennis Dever was a keeper at Boston Light in the late 1980s. Dever claimed that his radio used to change stations by itself, from rock music to classical music. He thought maybe the ghost of keeper George Worthylake was to blame.

This large foghorn made sound through a reed that was shaken by air that was compressed, or squeezed together.

The Coast Guard Takes Over

In 1939, the U.S. **Coast Guard** began to operate Boston Light. The keepers take turns living on the island for two weeks at a time. They have their homes on the mainland and can travel into Boston regularly. Unlike early lighthouse keepers, they call in reports of fog and other weather on the radio and have the equipment to respond quickly to emergencies. In 1998, the lighthouse was **automated**. This means that the light works by itself, and keepers no longer have to turn it on and off. Boston Light is the only lighthouse that still has keepers. In 1989, Congress decided that this lighthouse would remain "forever manned" as a tribute to all lighthouse keepers and American **maritime** history.

Visitors can climb stairs to the top of Boston Light for a view of the harbor.

Glossary

automated (AW-tuh-mayt-ed) When something operates on its own without help.

candlepower (KAN-duhl-pow-uhr) The amount of light coming from one candle.

cast-iron (KAST EYE-urn) Made of a mixture of iron and other elements that is heated until it melts into a liquid and is then poured into a mold.

channel (CHA-nuhl) A safe course ships use when entering or leaving a harbor.

coast guard (KOHST GARD) The part of a military that patrols the waters.

foundation (fown-DAY-shun) The base on which a structure is built.

Fresnel lens (FREZ-nehl LENZ) A lens named after its inventor, Augustin Fresnel.

inlets (IN-lets) Narrow waterways.

installed (in-STAHLD) To have set up for use.

kerosene (KAIR-uh-seen) A thin, colorless oil that is made from petroleum.

landmark (LAND-mark) A thing or place that is noticeable or worthy of notice.

lantern (LAN-turn) A covering or a container for a light.

legislature (LEH-jihs-lay-cher) A body of people that has the power to make or pass laws.

magnify (MAG-nih-fy) To cause light to appear stronger.

maritime (MAIR-ih-tym) Having to do with the sea.

navigational (nah-vuh-GAY-shuh-nul) Having to do with directing or figuring out the position of boats, ships, and aircraft.

prisms (PRIH-zumz) Solid objects made of glass, used to help reflect light.

reflectors (rih-FLEK-terz) Devices that throw back light or images.

sandbars (SAND-bahrz) Ridges or banks of sand in a river or bay, near the shore.

soot (SUT) Black powder that forms when things are burned.

War of 1812 (WOR UV ay-teen-TWELV) A war between the United States and Britain that lasted from 1812 to 1815.

Index

A

American Revolution, 10, 13
Argand lamps, 14

B

Boston Harbor, 5, 9

C

candlepower, 14
candles, 14
cannon, 9, 13

D

Dever, Dennis, 21

F

Fresnel, Augustin, 14
Fresnel lens, 13–14

G

Ghost Walk, 21

K

keeper(s), 17–18, 22

L

Little Brewster Island, 5, 17, 21

M

Massachusetts Bay, 5
merchants, 5

S

Saunders, Robert, 18

W

War of 1812, 10
Washington, George, 10
World War I, 10
World War II, 10
Worthylake, George, 18, 21

Web Sites

To learn more about Boston Light, check out these Web sites:

www.cr.nps.gov/maritime/nhl/boston.htm

www.lighthouse.cc/boston/history.html